What your 7-10 year old needs you to know about Anxiety

NICKY FORSTER

What your 7-10 year old needs you to know about Anxiety

PRACTICAL & SUSTAINABLE CHANGES YOU CAN START MAKING TODAY!

WRITTEN BY PARENTS FOR PARENTS

Contents

Introduction

Modern life has become difficult to lead. Our jobs have become demanding, and our schedules are hectic. Even our social life has become more competitive. In the rat race, it is difficult not to be anxious.

Unfortunately for the world, it's not just the adults who are stressed. More and more children show signs of severe anxiety these days, and the numbers keep increasing. In fact, an astounding number of children of all ages worldwide suffer from an anxiety disorder or feel anxious all the time.

What's even more frightening is that these are mainly children living perfectly happy lives who are still getting anxious about it. Everyday routines seem to push them into stress, and a lot of children seem too worried about the future to enjoy their present.

Even before the world changed with the Covid-19 pandemic, more than 5.6 million kids had been diagnosed with anxiety disorder. This alarming rate doesn't show any signs of decreasing any day soon; instead, the changing world has perhaps made our children more anxious.

My name is Nick, and my wife Rebecca and I have three children. Very recently, we moved houses, relocating across the country. Even more recently, we discovered that both our daughters - 9-year-old Alice and 7-year-old Lily - are struggling with anxiety to varying degrees. Alice has separation anxiety and is extremely worried about the changes in our daily routines, while Lily has severe trouble with sleeping at night. Suddenly faced with this serious problem, Rebecca and I wanted to learn how to help them get through their anxiety properly.

I've always known that my wife had anxiety. She had always struggled to cope, especially when she was a child/teenager. It was especially her - because she knows the pain and the uncertainty of anxiety disorder - and she didn't want our children to have the same experience.

For several months, we researched and talked to our friends about what our children were going through. We consulted a child psychologist so that we could have some understanding of anxiety disorder in children. Together, we made some sustainable changes around the house that helped our daughters feel more relaxed. Little by little, their anxiety became manageable. It took time and a lot of patience, but our daughters learned how to deal with this confusing world better.

However, we hadn't thought about writing a book on this topic. It was when we discovered that some of our friends were also struggling with anxious children that the idea finally came to us. I decided to write this book about how we dealt with our daughters' anxiety because I personally believe it will help a lot of parents out there.

Hopefully, this book will significantly help parents worried about their children having the same difficulties. Many things in our surroundings make our young children anxious and panicked, and as parents, I believe it is our responsibility to help them.

I've tried to be very practical while writing this book. I have talked about doable steps that can help your anxious child and simple actions that can reassure them. Throughout the four chapters of this book, I have pinpointed what makes young children anxious everywhere, what they feel inside, and how you can help them through these situations.

With young children, it is extremely difficult to understand what triggers them. As they grow up, their perception of the world changes with them constantly. What scared them yesterday might not seem like such a big deal tomorrow! Or they might suddenly be provoked by something they never even acknowledged!

Children between the ages of 7 to 10 are literally on the verge of becoming an individual. Almost overnight, they become harder to understand, moody, and easily agitated. They can become triggered by the simplest matters!

As I've seen from my own experience, this is also the age when some children develop severe anxiety. It could be something as simple as coming across a bug or as earth-shattering as fighting with their best friend.

Let me share a simple example here that will help you understand better.

Our 9-year-old, Alice, struggles with anxiety every time her routine at school changes. Small changes such as non-school uniform day, an impromptu school trip, a sports program, or any event when she is separated from her friends - her anxiety gets triggered. Seeing our daughter reacting negatively to these events when her friends were enjoying themselves was really hard for us. We couldn't predict her behaviour pattern, and with each simple change in our lives, our whole family prepared ourselves for a reaction.

With children of this age, there's really no telling how they'll react to something.

What you can do, however, is to help them when they're feeling anxious. That's where my book comes in.

Over the last couple of months, Rebecca and I have learned - through trial and error - how to deal with both our daughters, who are suffering from an anxiety disorder. From our extensive research and through trying different approaches, we have found some surefire ways to help children with anxiety disorder. That's exactly what I wanted to share with this book.

Good luck with reading this book, and good luck with your family.

Chapter 1

Important Signs of Anxiety Disorder

Remember your child's first day of school?

While some children sauntered up the stairs to preschool, confident and happy, others silently shed tears of anguish. Some throw tantrums, and others simply refuse to go inside. There will always be some children who can't wait to go to school and make new friends, but others become anxious simply at the thought.

Every child is different, and some children are more anxious than others. Children of all ages will show some form of anxiety over everything happening in their lives.

As parents, you must look for signs of severe anxiety that can become problematic later.

Regular Anxiety vs Anxiety Disorder
Even though we see some extremely confident and determined children around us, the truth is that anxiety is a common emotion in most children.

It is very regular for children to have **separation anxiety** up to 3 years of age. Preschoolers get clingy when they are separated from their parents, their loved ones, their carers, or even their favourite toys. Although it happens every day, they are known to cry and throw a tantrum whenever a parent leaves for work. The simple act of being separated from someone or something that they love, even for a little while, seems frightening to them.

A very young child having a problem with separation anxiety will show genuine fear, panic, and anxiousness when they are separated from a loved one. It's the same when they sense a separation coming in. Some children wake up in a bad mood in the morning because they know their parents will be heading off to work soon, and it takes years for this habit to break.

Intense fear or phobia of something specific is also common in young children, from dogs to monsters hiding inside the closet and bugs to aeroplanes. These phobias can continue well up to when a child becomes an adult but becomes more manageable with time. As with every person, having a phobia for something is completely natural in children, even when they are afraid of everyday things like knives or beetles.

Children aged 7 to 10, who are called both 'school-age children' or 'middle-age children', often develop **social anxiety** This kind of anxiety is also called 'social phobia', where many children grow an overwhelming fear of social situations. Although this particular anxiety is more common later during the teenage years, it is common for some younger children often show signs of it too.

Separation Anxiety, phobia, and social anxiety - are all common kinds of anxiety that children go through from a very young age until they grow up. Apart from these three types, some children are also known to go through **Post-Traumatic** tress Disorder (PTSD) after suffering a loss or a shock, panic isorder that occurs in children for no apparent reason, and lso **Obsessive-compulsive Disorder (OCD)** that can be seen in hildren as young as 3-4 years old.

However, in some cases, these anxieties become severe over .me and turn into an **anxiety disorder**.

The main difference between the regular anxiety that hildren experience every day and anxiety disorder is that the atter can ultimately hamper a child's daily life and regular ctions.

While anxiety - both for adults and children - is a normal art of our lives, anxiety disorder involves more. This kind of nxiety doesn't go away with age but can get worse with time.

nxiety Disorder: Recognizing the Signs

hildren are amazing when it comes to adaptability and change. hey might be paralyzed by fear of a dog one day and then beg or one the next month.

If your child seems anxious and fearful at times, it might imply be a part of growing up. Every child goes through these xtreme emotions at some point in their life. However, if the nxiety seems overwhelming, stopping them from functioning roperly or taking over the other parts of their lives, the situation ould be headed into an **anxiety disorder**.

Anxiety disorder has some specific signs to watch out for.

. Finding it Hard to Concentrate on Anything

" your child is anxious about everything, they'll have problems concentrating. This is a problem both at home and at school, as well as everywhere else. Fortunately, it's easy enough to spot this is a problem with your child.

Just like your child will be too excited to concentrate on anything before a birthday party or a trip, children with anxiety will show the same symptoms. While there might be a lot of other reasons for this, anxiety disorder is one of them.

According to neurologist Ken Schuster, PsyD, anxiety 'tends to lock up the brain' in children, which is why they have trouble focusing on anything. Because they are constantly worrying about one thing or another, anxious children can barely concentrate on their lessons, on the instructions being given to them, or on what everyone is saying around them. A huge part of their surrounding goes unnoticed because they are too busy worrying about something.

So when your child seems like they aren't listening to you or when they simply can't comprehend when the teacher is explaining their homework, it might be because they are anxious about something else.

2. Having Difficulty Sleeping or Waking up with Nightmares

Sometimes, your child might seem too agitated to sleep at night. They might constantly worry about school the next day, a test or their friends to be relaxed enough to sleep. The reason for getting agitated might be even simpler, like what clothes to wear the next day or if they'll be able to wake up on time the next morning. Although adults sometimes have the same problem, it's regular and severe in your child, it might be because of a anxiety disorder.

This is a sign we found in Lily, our 7-year-old. For months, she had trouble falling asleep at night, especially after we moved house. She needed to have at least one parent lie next to her when she tried to get to sleep. Without either of us there, she would get scared and have trouble chasing her 'horrible dreams' away. Even though she had a night light in her room, we were often woken by her visits late into the night because she needed us to put her back into bed.

Young children with separation anxiety often wake up in the middle of the night from vivid nightmares of their parents and loved ones dying. Again, this is something that happens to all human beings, but it is more serious in children.

3. Constantly Having Negative Thoughts about Everything.

'What if my friends don't come to my party?'

'They will come. All of their parents have confirmed.'

'What if they can't find the house?'

'Then they'll call me, and I'll give them directions.'

'What if they forget the date?'

'I'll remind them the night before.'

'What if they hate the party?'

This is what a typical conversation with an anxious child looks like!

With every explanation you give them, they'll develop more negative thoughts. It doesn't mean your child is being 'frustrating' or 'annoying'; this is just how their brain works when they're anxious about something.

4. Always Being Clingy and Crying without Explanation

There's a difference between a child who loves physical affection and one who is being clingy. A child with anxiety disorder belongs to the latter group, and there's a good reason behind that.

If your child is being overly clingy towards you, it is because they're nervous about being separated from you, even for a few minutes. It can be very draining for the parent if your child wants to stay attached to you 24/7, but they are like this because they are worried something might happen to you when you are not with them.

Clingy and anxious children also cry at the slightest provocation. They can also burst into tears without any apparent reason or explanation, and it usually takes a long time to calm them down. While there are many reasons for young children to cry - hunger, tiredness, discomfort, pain, or frustration being some of them - anxiety is an important one.

5. Constantly Tensing Up

A child who suffers from an anxiety disorder will show signs of physical discomfort when they have to face an unwanted situation. You can actually see your child physically tensing up when they face something they fear or are nervous about. This happens more if they have social anxiety issues or a phobia about something in particular.

Being nervous about something is completely different from being tense about it. You can be worrying about an upcoming presentation at work or an exam, but when you tense up in those situations, it will affect your performance. In the same way, your children can seem suddenly unable to speak or act because they are feeling anxious.

6. Throwing Tantrums and Acting Out

Throwing tantrums are quite common in young children, but if the tantrums become regular, it's not just your child being 'naughty' or 'seeking attention'. Sometimes, their anxious brain, which is always in a 'fight or flight mode', senses danger in certain situations and starts acting up.

For children who are already suffering from anxiety, any situation that's unfamiliar to them, uncomfortable, or difficult to deal with becomes a threat. They respond to it by throwing a tantrum, which can usually be misinterpreted as attention-seeking behaviour. But the truth is, when faced with a difficult situation, your child isn't trying to be a nuisance. They are simply trying to deal with it in the only manner they know how.

7. Not Eating Properly or Complaining of Stomach Ache

This is actually a very visible sign of your child going through a problem: they'll have a diminished appetite and regularly complain of stomach pains.

Between the ages of 7 and 10, any healthy child will be extremely active and have a voracious appetite. Their bodies and minds require a lot of nutrition at that age, and any child could be seen demanding food every half an hour. However, if your child seems to have lost their appetite, it could be because they are anxious about something.

Most children also complain of their stomach hurting and

a general feeling of unwell. This is also a common side effect of them being nervous or dreading something. You might also know these feelings as 'butterflies in our stomach' or our 'stomach churning' when you are anxious about something. Children, on the other hand, will complain about having stomach pains and make frequent trips to the toilet.

There you have it!

Crying, being clingy, throwing tantrums, complaining of stomach aches, having nightmares, always thinking of negative consequences, having trouble concentrating on anything, and having trouble sleeping - all these are classic signs that your child is suffering from an anxiety disorder.

While we may dismiss them as a part of growing up or looking for attention, the underlying problem can be much bigger. Therefore, if your child is showing some or all of these signs regularly, they might be suffering from anxiety disorder and need help.

Chapter 2

What Your Child Wants You to Understand

s easy to dismiss your child's problems as naughtiness or mething they would eventually grow out of. As parents, you can nore all the times they have seemed nervous about absolutely thing or acted strange over trifle matters. In fact, most parents ink their child will automatically stop being anxious one day.

However, if your child is suffering from an anxiety disorder, is simply impossible for them to naturally 'grow out of it' one y. It doesn't happen that way.

Children between the ages of 7 to 10 are extremely lnerable, and when they find themselves anxious over the mplest things, they need their parents' help. So if your child having some problems with their anxiety, you need to step up d help them.

In order to help your child, you'll need to understand them st.

Understanding the Reasons Behind Their Anxiety

Unfortunately, some children are born more anxious tha others; they are less able to cope with problems and stress. Eve when they become adults, it is difficult for them to let go of the anxiety, although they may learn to manage it somehow.

Other children pick up the behaviour if the people aroun them are nervous all the time. If one of their parents or a clos loved one has an anxiety order, young children can pick up th behavioural pattern from them.

However, most of the time, young school-going childre develop anxiety disorder after some major changes i their life or after they've been through a stressful even

Most children feel stressed after events such as:

- **Having to move houses.** Moving is a huge deal for your children. While moving houses, neighbourhoods or citie may indicate positive changes in the parents' lives, fc children, it means leaving behind a safe environmen In most cases it also means leaving behind the enti neighbourhood and friends, which makes children fe stressed.
- **Changing schools.** Sometimes, moving homes also mean changing schools and leaving behind friends and teacher This can be stressful for anyone, let alone a child. In som cases, if your child already has trouble making new friend it will be extra stressful for them to do so again in a ne school.

- **Going through traumatic events.** Bullying affects everyone differently. While some children can handle being bullied and even answer back, others are more stressed about it. If your child is being bullied at school, this can be one of the major reasons for their anxiety. If your child refuses to go to school or becomes anxious at the thought of going to school, this can be one of the reasons.
- **Struggling with their work.** If your child is struggling with their school work, music lessons, sports team, or anything else they consider an important part of their education; it is common for them to feel anxious about it. They might also feel overwhelmed by their work or because they can't cope with the pressure.
- **Feeling Family Stress.** If the parents or any other family member is going through any kind of stress - financial, health-related, emotional, or mental - it is normal for the children to feel anxious about it, too. Sometimes parents discuss such topics in front of their children, which can directly affect them, or they can sense the unhappy emotions in the house and feel anxious about it.
- **Observing Marital Problems.** Very young children are known to feel anxious whenever they hear their parents fighting, even when it is a simple argument. On the other hand, if marital problems between the parents are extreme, it certainly raises a child's stress level. Many children develop an anxiety disorder when their parents get divorced; sometimes, they start to worry about the state of their own parents' marriage when a friend's

parents are splitting up.

- **Experiencing a Death.** The death of a loved one, or even someone they know vaguely, can be devastating for a child. If your child has recently experienced death or if someone close to them has passed away recently, their anxiety can be a result of that. For children, the death of a loved one makes them constantly anxious about their parent's life and well-being.

- **Being Abused or Molested.** If your child suddenly seems anxious but is reluctant to discuss it with you, the underlying reason can be quite serious. If a child has recently been abused or molested by someone, they might develop an anxiety disorder. Instead of talking about it or notifying their parents, abused or molested children become extremely stressed and withdraw from everyone else.

- **Becoming Ill or Surviving an Accident.** In this unfair world, even children aren't spared complicated illnesses or accidents. If your child has recently experienced something like this, it's normal that they'd be anxious for a long time afterwards.

Besides all these reasons, severe anxiety can be a symptom of Attention Deficit Hyperactivity Disorder (ADHD) or Autistic Spectrum Disorder in young children.

Just like there are different kinds of anxiety disorders that your child can develop, the reasons behind them can be many. If you see symptoms of severe anxiety in your children, as parents the first thing to do would be to look for the reasons behind them

How can this help?

When you know exactly why your child is feeling anxious, you can help them better. **By understanding their reason, you can understand your child better.**

Not all anxieties are the same, and the reasons play a significant part in helping your child with their feelings. When you can pinpoint the exact reasons your child has developed anxiety - suddenly or gradually - it takes you one step closer to helping them.

Understanding how your Children Feel when they're Anxious

Anxiety is your body's answer to any kind of physical danger or mental threat, a symptom of your inbuilt 'flight-or-fight' response. In both children and adults, whenever you feel something threaten your well-being, your body becomes anxious.

Anxiety usually hits when you experience certain events, but with some people, it is a constant part of their lives. It is especially evident in childhood because some people are simply born that way. Children who develop anxiety disorders suffer from the symptoms for a long time, even after growing up.

With time, adults learn to rationalize their anxiety. We understand what we feel, why we feel these emotions, and how they affect our lives. Because we're adults, we learn to deal with them eventually. It's much more difficult for children.

Ages 7 to 10 is a transitional time for children. They go through many new experiences every day: making new friends, learning new subjects at school, learning to swim, and playing a sport. For them, every day brings a new adventure, a step towards growing up.

Unfortunately, not all children react the same to these adventures. Some children often feel a mixture of complex emotions when facing something new. It can be quite stressful for them, even when it's a good thing they're facing. While other children are excited to try something new, these anxious children worry too much about handling them.

'Am I ready for this?'

'Will I enjoy it?'

'What if people don't like it?'

'Is it safe for me to do this?'

'Do my friends really like me?'

'Am I really good at this?'

These are the kind of questions that always pester their minds.

While other children are off enjoying everything life brings them, the more nervous children are worrying about the consequences and coming up with every negative outcome possible. Sometimes it's genetic; at other times, it's because of their environment or because of a shock they've received recently. One thing is for certain: children with an anxiety disorder can rarely enjoy something completely.

Anxiety is just the tip of the iceberg you see from the outside. For a child, there are dozens of underlying experiences and emotions that they are dealing with

- Embarrassment,
- Shame,

18

- Overwhelmedness,
- Helplessness,
- Insecurity,
- Uncomfortableness,
- Fear,
- Depression,
- Frustration,
- Confusion,
- Sadness,
- Hurt,
- Regret,
- Rejection, and
- Loneliness

nd these are just some of the emotions a child goes through
multaneously, even when they're about to embark on an
mazing adventure.

Imagine your parents hosting a birthday party for you and
ou worrying about it going well to truly enjoy it! Imagine going
Disneyland for the first time and being anxious about whether
will really meet your expectations!

That's how anxiety works for your children.

If your child has an anxiety disorder, it is crucial for you
understand how they feel. Sometimes, their behaviour may
em excessive even to the parents. You might, unconsciously,
ll them to 'just stop worrying for one minute' or 'lighten up and
op spoiling everyone's moods' to salvage the situation. You'll
ily be making the matter worse with this kind of response.

However, you must understand that some children don behave like this voluntarily. It's in their nature to worry; the can't help but worry about everything.

As parents, when you understand this, you'll be able to hel them deal with their anxiety better.

Understanding Your Negative Role in Their Anxiety

As parents or caregivers, you might be enabling your child anxiety disorder. Have you ever stopped to think about that?

No parent wants their child to worry all the time, but yo may just as well be the reason behind your children's anxiet This is because anxiety is a hereditary disorder, and in mo: cases, an anxious child is a direct result of one or both paren being natural worriers themselves.

Unfortunately, this cannot be helped because there nothing you can do about your genetic traits.

What you can do, however, is to take a look at your ow behaviour. Whether you, too, are anxious by nature or simp worried about your child's anxiety, your behaviour might refle what you're feeling inside. If your child witnesses this, you anxiety will only worsen the situation.

It is entirely possible that you are, directly or indirectl responsible for your child's anxiety. If you are enabling the behaviour either by showing your anxiety or by mirroring their it's the wrong route to take. Witnessing a parent's anxiety will t unsettling for your child. Despite your best intention, you migl be causing your child to be more anxious in certain situations.

As parents, therefore, it is crucial to observe how your ow

behaviour is enabling your child's anxiety disorder.

In order to help your child's anxiety disorder, you must first understand it. This means understanding the reasons behind their anxiety, what they're feeling inside, and your role in the matter. Only when you get into the depth of the matter can you think of the perfect ways to help your child deal with their feelings.

That's what we're going to discuss in the next chapter.

Chapter 3

What Your Child Needs From You

When your child struggles with anxiety and doesn't know how to cope with the world, who will they come to? You. Their parents. The people who love them unconditionally and will stick by them no matter what.

As parents of anxious children, we always want our children to be happy. We want them to feel secure in their environment and be able to deal with whatever comes their way. We want the world for them, but it's not enough unless we know exactly what to do.

What do Children with Anxiety Disorder Need from You?
Having a child with anxiety disorder means dealing with someone who hasn't quite figured out how to deal with the world. Even the simplest things worry them to the point where they can't function properly.

As painful as it is to admit, these children really, really need your help.

There are, actually, several ways that you can help your child deal with anxiety. Whether they seem overwhelmed by something, they're having an anxiety attack, or are troubled by something they don't understand properly; parents can help a lot simply by being there and doing the right things.

Remember, the wrong approach can make things worse and make your anxious child even more so. If you find your child in doubt and difficulty, you must say the right things at the right moment.

To explain this better, here's a list of ways to approach your anxious child.

1. Stay Calm and Reasonable the Whole Time

No matter how anxious your child is feeling, you cannot react. Even when you feel wretched and helpless on the inside, you must maintain a calm and serene facade on the outside. It is crucial for you to do so if you want your child to calm down eventually.

So the moment that you feel your child is heading toward an anxiety attack or if they seem overwhelmed about something, fix your own reaction to the event. Force yourself to appear calm even though it's miles away from what you're feeling on the inside. It will give your child the courage to face up to the situation and give you the patience to deal with it.

2. Acknowledge their Anxiety

Even when you can't see the reason behind it, your child's worries are real. What they're feeling inside is real, and they need you to acknowledge it. When you're absolutely sure nothing bad is going to happen in the future, it is still important that you listen to your child's fear about it and acknowledge how they're feeling about it. Sometimes, that's all they need from you.

What good is acknowledgement when you can't help them with something? The warmth, compassion, and acceptance that your child will hear in your voice when you agree with them over their fears will give them the strength they need.

When Alice, my 9-year-old, started panicking about one of her teachers getting replaced for the term, we tried listening to her whenever she was in the mood to vent. We didn't offer her our wisdom ('changes are a big part of our life') or hope ('maybe the new teacher would be even better') because we felt that she needed to make sense of the situation herself. We listened and nodded, and we acknowledged that, yes, this is 'very hurtful that her teacher can simply leave one day'.

Slowly, after she was done venting, Alice came to terms with the problem herself. She started to like her new teacher and gradually forgot the entire problem. We didn't have to do much in this regard except listen to her and acknowledge her problem because that was all she needed from us at the moment.

3. Explore the Negative Feeling With Them

Ask your child what is happening, what's bothering them, and how they are feeling on the inside. Using your calmest voice, ask them to explain their feelings but don't pressure them. If they don't want to talk about the topic at that moment, don't insist on it.

When your child is anxious, let them use their own words to describe what's happening in their mind. Don't assume anything, and don't supply the words when they falter or when ney're confused. If they are willing to talk but can't find th words, prompt them with questions such as:

'How do you feel?'

'What might be the reason for this feeling?'

'How long do you think the feeling is going to last?'

'Why do you think you're feeling this way?'

'What will make you feel better?'

'What can I do to help?'

Be calm and confident when you remind them that this elpless feeling will eventually pass and that you'll help them rough it all.

Show them that you Understand

he worst thing you can do for your child when they're feeling nxious is to undermine their emotions. Saying 'it's nothing' or lling them to 'stop looking for attention' will only make them shamed of their feelings, and they'll have a hard time opening p to you in the future.

On the other hand, the best thing you can do at that moment to let your child know that you 'understand'. That's the magic ord that your child wants to hear from you.

'I understand what you're feeling right now.'

'I understand that you're feeling a lot of emotions.'

'I understand that you're feeling scared, and it is making ou anxious.'

'I understand what you are going through at the moment, nd I want to help.'

By simply letting your child know that you understand what

they're going through, you're acknowledging their feelings. By telling them that you understand, you're encouraging them to share their thoughts with you, and this will work wonders.

5. Ask them to Share their Worries

Don't tell your child not to think about their worries; don't tell them to forget their worries or to stop thinking about them. This won't help them because it's neither a supportive approach nor a validating one. They won't be able to get rid of their worries or stop thinking about what's bothering them, even when you urge them to.

Instead, start a conversation with them regarding what's worrying them. Ask them questions and encourage them to share their concerns about the topic. Even if you can't offer a solution at the moment, just by showing interest and listening to them, you'll be helping your child to relax.

Simply by discussing their worries, you'll be helping your child to reduce the amount of anxiety they are feeling inside. Talking about it will also help you understand what's going on in your child's mind, and you'll be able to come up with a better solution for them.

6. Support them Without Being Controlling

There's a huge difference between being supportive and being controlling, and you cannot be the latter.

As parents, it is your job to protect your child, but you cannot be overprotective, shielding them from everything. If you eliminate a problem even before it becomes a trigger for your child, they won't get the opportunity to handle it. Life will keep throwing problems at your family, and while you can soften the blows and help your child navigate through them, you can't eliminate them all.

Supporting your child means listening to them, acknowledging their fears, holding their hands as they navigate their fears, and encouraging them all the way. That's the right way to help their anxiety disorder.

However, if you are eliminating all the problems beforehand and you're creating a safe environment for them, you're also taking away the chance to learn. Your child doesn't need that from you.

7. Encourage some Brave Behaviors in them

Apart from supporting them, your child will sometimes need that small nudge in the right direction. This means helping them set small, achievable goals regarding something they're anxious about.

Remember, this is not about pushing your child to do something they're uncomfortable with or anxious about. You cannot nag them or pester them about something they're not ready to start. Instead, give them small and specific tasks that might not seem too hard.

When Lily, our 7-year-old, first started attending school, she was worried about making friends. Besides listening to her fears ('Yes,, I can see why that would worry you') and asking her to explore her feelings ('Why do you think you're worried about that?'), we also gently nudged her with small steps every other

27

day.

'Why don't you try saying 'hi' to someone today?'

'How about you tell someone you like their bag today?'

'Can you ask someone if you can sit beside them today?'

'Today, why don't you ask someone about their favourite snack?'

Every now and then, we prompted her to do something small until she became confident enough to start talking to the other children in the class.

So as you can see, it's not always enough to watch from the shadows. Sometimes, you'll need to give them a little nudge in the right direction.

A huge part of knowing how to deal with your anxious child is knowing what to say to them, how to react, and taking the right steps to help them. You need to remember that your child's anxiety is a long-term process, and you need to be patient to help them through it. With constant effort and knowing precisely what to do in every situation, you can help to manage their anxiety.

Chapter 4

Make Sustainable Changes around the House

When your child suffers from an anxiety disorder, the entire world is a constant source of worry for them. Their school can confuse them, their friends can misunderstand them, other people can be hard to interpret, and their teachers can quickly lose patience with them.

So while the rest of the world confuses and worries your child, you must create a safe environment for them at home.

Creating a safe environment at home for your anxious child means paying attention to two main aspects of your life: a stable routine and healthy habits.

As parents with young children in the house, it is important for every family to practice good habits at home. However, when your child has an anxiety disorder, it becomes more important for you to stick to them.

In this chapter, I'll discuss how we established a stable daily routine at home and the healthy habits that we follow strictly, especially with our two daughters.

Start by Eating Healthy

We all know the basics of eating healthy: no processed food, limited carbs, lots of proteins, fruits, and vegetables. However it's not so easy to do this with children.

It is quite natural that your children will sulk for the occasional cola or chips even when you've explained their negative impacts for hours. You can't really deny them cakes or chocolates for special occasions either because that would be cruel. The moment that they're out of sight, you can be sure they'll be gulping down sugar and caffeinated drinks at their friend's house.

Keeping all that in mind, we still try to eat healthily at our house. Our meal plans are simple, and they're the same for everyone. As a general rule, we try to avoid anything that's processed or too sugary, but there are some foods and drinks that we avoid altogether in our diet

- Fried or deep-fried foods;
- Full-fat milk and butter;
- Baked goods;
- White bread;
- Ready-made microwave meals;
- Frozen foods; and
- Any store-bought cookies.

It might seem hard at first, but it'll be a great decision not just for you but for your entire family if you can also avoid these foods.

At the same time, there are some special nutrition, foods

nd drinks that will help your child to feel less anxious all the
me.

1. **Yoghurt** is indispensable for gut health; a healthy gut leads
   to a healthy and happy mind. The probiotics in yoghurt
   help to reduce behaviours that are associated with anxiety,
   stress, and depression.

2. There's a reason that **turkey** meat is so popular as a holiday
   main; it causes people to relax naturally. It is also very
   effective in reducing stress and anxiety in children. In our
   home, we've replaced most of our protein needs with turkey
   meat.

3. **Eggs** have always been a part of our daily breakfast for our
   kids and us. Lately, we learned that eggs are a storehouse
   of Vitamin B, the deficiency of which causes children to
   become irritable, confused, and anxious.

4. **Foods high in magnesium,** such as **pumpkin seeds, flax
   seeds, and sunflower seeds,** are also great when your child
   is anxious. Since our children aren't exactly fans of seeds as
   snacks, we often sneak them inside their food.

5. Ever since discovering our daughters' anxiety disorder,
   we researched and replaced all our carbs with **complex
   carbohydrates,** which include **quinoa, oatmeal, whole-
   grain cereals and whole-grain bread**. We couldn't be
   happier with the results since complex carbohydrates make
   you feel fuller and keep the kids more active.

6. Like all other children, my daughters weren't very fond of
   fish, but we still introduced **fishes rich in Omega-3, such as
   salmon and cod**, into our daily meals.

7. We have also included **vegetables and beans rich in folat and zinc** in our meals, such as **asparagus, chickpea black and kidney beans, spinach, edamame, lentils, an romaine.**

8. Fortunately, our kids have always loved fruits, so we'v added some more **fruits high in fibre**, like **mangoe oranges, bananas, strawberries, raspberries, and apple to their snacks.**

9. We have also found tricks to sneak **high-fibre vegetable such as spinach, leafy greens, carrots, beets, brocco and artichokes** into their omelettes, pasta, and soups.

10. Finally, we've replaced all kinds of sodas, fruit drinks, an energy drinks in our home with **room-temperature wate** Dehydration is one of the biggest reasons children fe anxious throughout the day; even mild dehydration ca affect them. So, we try to keep our daughters hydrated wi large glasses of water every hour.

Maintain Regular Sleep Hours

Besides their nutrition, regular and deep sleep is just as importa for children with anxiety disorder. Fortunately for us, this is al something that we can ensure for our kids.

The key here is to ensure your child gets the required numb of daily sleep hours and to ensure their sleep is uninterrupte and peaceful. This is harder for anxious children because the have trouble falling asleep at night and also because they ha more nightmares than others.

Even a few months ago, a good sleep routine was a hu

problem for our 7-year-old. My wife Rebecca and I went through many trial-and-error decisions for months trying to get our daughter to settle down for the night. Here is a list of some of the tricks that ultimately worked for our family.

1. **Keep their bedtime fixed.** Your children should have a fixed bedtime every day, which no one can change under any circumstances. Even on the weekends, it is better to stick to their bedtime as much as possible. After a few days of practice, this will automatically make them sleepy when bedtime approaches. We tried this technique, and all three of our kids would automatically start yawning half an hour before their respective bedtime. It was their body and their brain that were signalling them to get ready for bed.

2. **Practice a specific bedtime routine every day.** Dinner, board games, bath, changing into PJs, brushing their teeth, and then off to bed - that's the specific bedtime routine we all follow in our family. It does not just help the children feel ready for bedtime, but the routine's monotony and repetitiveness actually lull them to sleep sooner than they intended.

3. **Your job is to put your child to bed, but they must self-regulate their sleep.** Your responsibility as a parent doesn't require you to force your children to sleep but only to ensure they're ready and in bed by bedtime. Reminding them repeatedly that 'they have school tomorrow' or that 'they'll be tired tomorrow if they don't sleep immediately' will make them more anxious. In our family, we avoid pressuring the kids to fall asleep. Rather,

we create a comfortable environment for them in their bedroom where they can fall asleep independently.

4. **Spend some time with them before sleep.** In our family, we spend half an hour before our children's bedtime together. Sometimes we read together; other times, we simply cuddle and talk. My wife and I tell them about our childhood or our day at work, and they talk to us about school. If they feel anxious about falling asleep, we help them relax by spending some quality time together before bedtime.

5. **It is very important that you mind their fluid intake.** We discourage the children from drinking any water after bedtime since it leads to restless sleep. Also, they must visit the toilet before getting into bed so that there's no midnight trip either.

6. **Don't allow any screen time before bed.** While our kids are allowed television in the afternoon, we try to keep all screens off completely at least two hours before bedtime. We've had great results with this rule. Not just the children, we also keep our screens off before bedtime and spend the time as a family instead.

7. **Give them the bedroom they want.** Since your child is going to sleep in the room, it should ideally be exactly what they want. The colours, the ambience, their choice of cartoons, a bed they've selected themselves, the artwork of their choice etc. - everything should follow your child's preferences. A nightlight helps my daughters feel safer in their rooms, and sometimes, we even keep the door ajar instead of shut if that's what they want.

8. Get them a security object. Many children prefer to sleep with a beloved toy, doll, or blanket, and there's nothing childish about it. Even we adults have a specific pillow or a blanket that makes us feel comfortable at night. Both our daughters sleep with dolls they've had since they were babies, and we encourage this behaviour. Their dolls give them comfort and a feeling of safety, and they sleep better when they're clutching their dolls at night.

t is almost crucial that your anxious child has a proper night's sleep every day. Otherwise, their anxiety will increase if they haven't rested well the night before. A child who has slept poorly or been disturbed several times during the night by a nightmare is - in our experience - more prone to be restless and anxious all day.

Maintain Discipline and a Steady Routine

Although children may seem to detest routine, they actually prefer to have a structured life. Our kids want us to tell them what to do and what not to do, and they constantly need both the guidance and the discipline that we can provide for them. In fact, children need a sense of routine and a definite plan for their day to feel emotionally regulated.

In our family, we have always maintained a routine for meals, sleep, family time, television, chores, and homework. Even when the children were little, we had a visual routine hanging in the living room that they could easily follow. Our daughters still find it easier to deal with the day when they know exactly what they have to do every single hour. It might seem stifling to others, but that's actually how an anxious child feels better.

The weekends are slightly more relaxed, but they are still structured. We allow them more free play time on the weekends, but they still have fixed timing for chores and TV. Sometimes they complain about having to do chores on the weekends, but we've found this rule to work perfectly in our family.

Introduce Physical Exercise

Physical games, running around in the yard, jogging, household chores, dancing, even roughhousing between siblings - any kind of physical exercise is known to stimulate certain chemicals in our body and make us feel good. In children, too, the same chemicals can treat their anxious feelings.

For this reason, we encourage a lot of exercising in our family. This doesn't mean that we spend hours at the gym, but we choose physically demanding games as a family. All three of our kids play a sport, but we also like to dance together to music on our days off. We plan long walks as a family, ride our bikes together, and take long walks with the whole family. Most of the time, we simply spend time under the sun while the kids just run around playing with each other.

Since Alice has always been nervous before going to school, we discovered that riding their bikes to school has helped both of our daughters tremendously. Fortunately, it was possible for us, as we live close enough to their school for them to bike to it. I realise it's not going to be so easy for other families, but we've found it to be helpful for my daughters.

We've found all this exercise miraculous for our daughters, specially when they seem a little anxious. Running around in the afternoon also leads to a good night's sleep and fewer nightmares, so this is definitely something we recommend personally.

Create a Safe Environment for Them to Communicate

Communication is key in every relationship, but more so when you're dealing with an anxious child. Since the whole world confuses and even scares your child, they need a safe space where they can talk to you about anything. This can come in many forms: a special time for them to worry, a specific task you share with them, or a physical space where they go when they want to talk to you.

When we first realised that Alice, our 9-year-old, was suffering from anxiety, we gave her a special time of the day that was her 'worry hour'. It was an hour after dinner, a few hours before she would go to bed. Alice would find either or both of us when it was her 'worry hour,' and she could freely talk about anything and everything that was bothering her. It could be something that happened at school, something her teacher said that confused her, or even a disagreement with her friends. Although we always try to listen to our children when they want to talk to us, Alice's 'worry hour' is a time when she knows that she has our full attention.

Alternatively, you can create a physically safe space for your child, one they can use whenever they feel anxious. It can be a corner of a room, their very own playroom that they decorate themselves, or a tent where they can rest when they need some comfort. Give them the independence to decorate the space wit their favourite toys, books, music, pillows, or blankets - anythin that helps them calm down. This is a great idea because if you child feels anxious in your absence, they'll have a safe space t retreat to.

A huge part of helping your child cope with anxiety mear making certain changes around them. This includes sma changes like limiting caffeine and sugar in your home to larg changes, i.e. creating fixed routines and teaching your childre to cope with negative emotions. However, all these big and sma steps are necessary if you want your children to feel safer a home, more confident, and comfortable in their skin.

Conclusion

It's been 18 months since we discovered that our eldest, Alice, suffered from an anxiety disorder. Perhaps it was always a part of her personality since my wife Rebecca also suffers from it. Not long after, our second daughter Lily also started showing signs of anxiety disorder.

The last one-and-a-half years have been extremely difficult for us. We've researched everything we could in relation to anxiety disorder in children, consulted professionals, and discussed the problem with our friends. We've tried everything we could to ensure that we're taking the right approach to deal with our daughters.

I'm absolutely sure that we're not alone in this. Just like us, there must be millions of parents out there who are in the same boat at this moment, confused about what to do with our children suffering from an anxiety disorder. When I decided to write this book, we were only thinking of the parents we could help with our experience and information.

I am not a professional, and I am definitely not an expert on this topic. What you found in this book was just the thoughts and ideas of a parent like you. If my experience of the last one-and-a-half years can help your journey in any way, that'll be my greatest reward.

Printed in Great Britain
by Amazon

43475112R00030